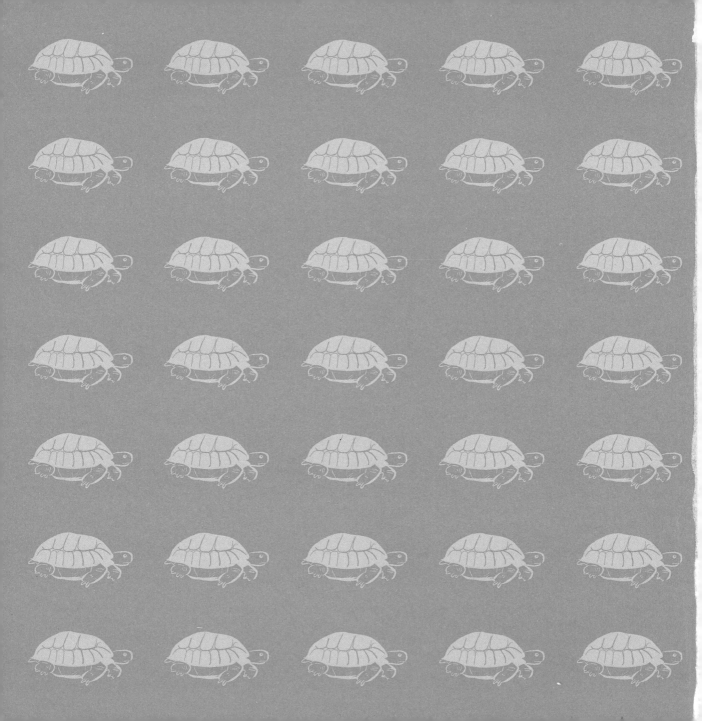

I am
Abraham Lincoln

BRAD MELTZER

illustrated by Christopher Eliopoulos

DIAL BOOKS FOR YOUNG READERS an imprint of Penguin Group (USA) LLC

I am **Abraham Lincoln.**

I also loved animals.
When I was ten years old, I saw a group
of boys playing with some turtles.

But as I got closer, I realized they weren't *playing*. They were taking hot coals and putting them on top of the turtles, to see what would happen. To them, it was harmless fun.

In that moment, I could have just walked away.
When you're ten years old, it's hard to do the right thing.
But someone has to.

Those boys let the turtle go.

Soon after, I wrote one of my first essays—about how hurting animals is wrong.

That may not seem like a big deal, but back then, most kids—and even adults—didn't know how to write.

In fact, the state of Indiana was so new, schools weren't even built yet.

I went to school for barely a year. *Total!*
But that didn't stop me.
Using chalk, I practiced writing the
alphabet on trees.
I even wrote in the dirt of the cornfield.

When it came to learning, my best teachers were simply . . . *books*.

I loved books so much, I once walked six miles (I'm serious—six miles!) to get one.

I'd read while my horse was resting.

And while waiting in line at the local store.

And in one of my favorite positions: with my feet up on a tree.

Before long, I had read every book in the neighborhood, from the Bible to *Aesop's Fables* to *Robinson Crusoe*.
But one of my favorites? A book about George Washington.

Today some may call it a fight, but it was really a wrestling match.

Me against their leader, Jack Armstrong.

Back then the rule was, once you grabbed your opponent, you couldn't break your hold.

But Jack did . . . so he could grab my leg and send me flying.

I wasn't mad I lost. Everyone loses sometimes.
What got me upset?
He had *cheated*!

Sometimes, the hardest fights don't reveal a winner—
but they do reveal character.
Especially when you're fighting for something you believe in.

Still, not every struggle brought a victory.
Years later, I saw a group of slaves chained together in a boat on the Ohio River.
Back then, not all people were free.
Some were slaves.

Just because of the color of their skin, they were forced to work without pay. They were treated terribly.

I never forgot the sight of that boat.

I didn't do anything that day, but for years, the memory of those people . . . it haunted me.

I was still thinking about them when I became president.

I lost four elections before I got the big job. Four!

America was facing one of the greatest fights in our history: the Civil War.

One side wanted to let the slaves go free.

The other side . . .

If I had turned my head and looked away,
I would've avoided the fight.
   But if I'd learned anything in life,
it was this:
   When someone needed help,
I wasn't so good at looking away.

The Civil War lasted longer than anyone thought.
The fighting took a terrible toll.
People on our side were ready to give up.
To reenergize them, we held a big event in Gettysburg, Pennsylvania.

Soon after, I helped pass a law that ended slavery in America and freed all those people.
Then we ended the Civil War.

As a result, we didn't just bring together these United States of America—we proved that this government of the people, by the people, and for the people would be dedicated to freedom and justice.

In life, strength can take many forms. But there's nothing quite as strong as standing up for someone who needs it.

No matter where you're from, or how little you have, one thing that can never be taken away from you is your *voice*.

When you find something you believe in, use your voice.

And when you see injustice, speak louder than you've ever spoken before.

When you do . . .

I am Abraham Lincoln.
I will never stop fighting for what's right.
And I hope you'll remember that when you
speak your mind—and speak for others—
there's no more powerful way to be heard.

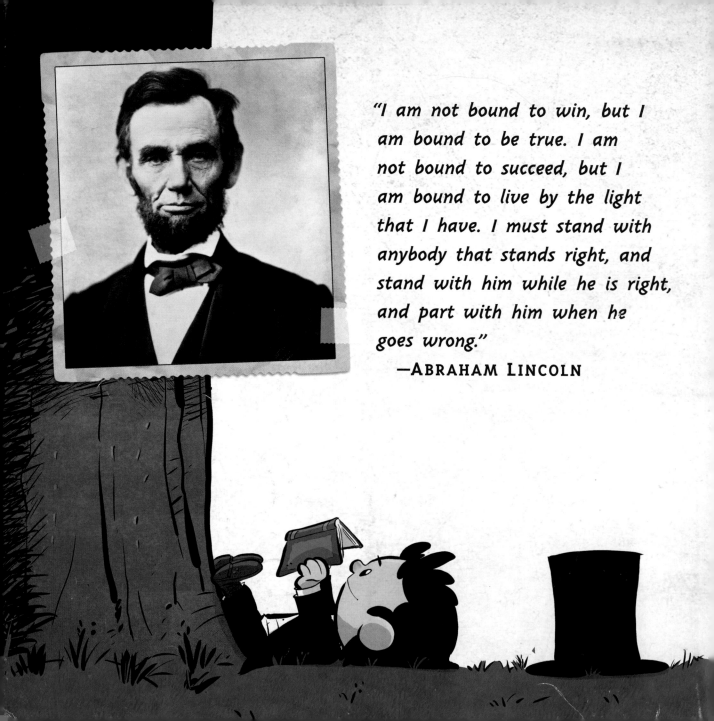

"I am not bound to win, but I am bound to be true. I am not bound to succeed, but I am bound to live by the light that I have. I must stand with anybody that stands right, and stand with him while he is right, and part with him when he goes wrong."

—ABRAHAM LINCOLN

During the Civil War, 1862

Replica of Abraham's first home, found at the Lincoln Birthplace National Historical Park in Kentucky

Giving the Gettysburg Address, 1863

For Theo & Jonas,
my sons,
may you always fight for what's right,
and for those who need it
—B.M.

For Jeremy & Justin.
Always be strong by helping the weak,
always stand up for those who can't speak,
and even though you're identical,
you will always be unique.
—Dad (C.E.)

Special thanks to Douglas L. Wilson and the Lincoln Studies Center
at Knox College in Illinois

DIAL BOOKS FOR YOUNG READERS
Published by the Penguin Group • Penguin Group (USA) LLC, 375 Hudson Street, New York, New York 10014

USA | Canada | UK | Ireland | Australia | New Zealand | India | South Africa | China
penguin.com

A PENGUIN RANDOM HOUSE COMPANY

Text copyright © 2014 by Brad Meltzer • Illustrations copyright © 2014 by Christopher Eliopoulos

Library of Congress Cataloging-in-Publication Data
Meltzer, Brad. • I am Abraham Lincoln/Brad Meltzer; illustrated by Christopher Eliopoulos. • pages cm. — (Ordinary people change the world)
ISBN 978-0-8037-4083-9 (hardcover: acid-free paper) • 1. Lincoln, Abraham, 1809–1865—Juvenile literature. 2. Presidents—United States—
Biography—Juvenile literature. 3. United States—History—Civil War, 1861–1865—Juvenile literature. 4. United States—Politics and government—1861–1865—
Juvenile literature. I. Eliopoulos, Christopher, illustrator. II. Title. • E457.905.M45 2014 973.7092—dc23 [B] 2013016424

Photograph of Abraham Lincoln on page 38, image of Lincoln giving the Gettysburg Address on page 39, and photo in front of a tent (on the battlefield of
Antietam) on page 39 courtesy of the Library of Congress • Cabin photo on page 39 from the Abraham Lincoln Birthplace National Historical Park
in Hodgenville, Kentucky, courtesy of the Library of Congress

Manufactured in China on acid-free paper • 10 9 8 7 6 5 4 3 2 1
Designed by Jason Henry • Text set in Triplex • The artwork for this book was created digitally.

The publisher does not have any control over and does not assume any responsibility for author or third-party websites or their content.

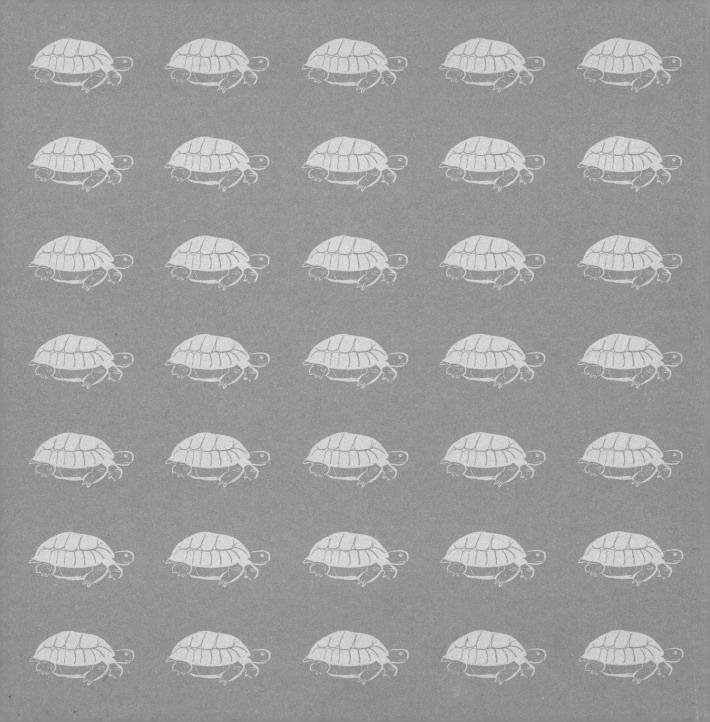